P9-BZB-457

POETRY

by Laura Purdie Salas

Compass Point Books ✦ Minneapolis, Minnesota

Compass Point Books
3109 West 50th Street, #115
Minneapolis, MN 55410

 This book was manufactured with paper containing
at least 10 percent post-consumer waste.

Managing Editor: Catherine Neitge
Page Production: Bobbie Nuytten
Photo Researcher: Svetlana Zhurkin

Creative Director: Keith Griffin
Editorial Director: Nick Healy

Compass Point Books would like to acknowledge the contributions of Tish Farrell, who
authored earlier Write Your Own books and whose supporting text is reused in part herein.

Library of Congress Cataloging-in-Publication Data
Salas, Laura Purdie.
  Write your own poetry / by Laura Purdie Salas.
     p. cm. — (Write your own)
Includes index.
ISBN 978-0-7565-3519-3 (library binding)
1. Poetry—Authorship—Juvenile literature. I. Title. II. Series.
PN1059.A9S35 2008
808.1—dc22   2007033096

Visit Compass Point Books on the Internet at *www.compasspointbooks.com*
or e-mail your request to *custserv@compasspointbooks.com*

About the Author
Laura Purdie Salas loves to write poetry. She is the author
of 11 forthcoming poetry collections, including *And Then
There Were Eight: Poems About Space*. She has also written
more than 35 nonfiction books for kids. Laura grew up
in Florida and moved to Minnesota, where she lives with
her husband, two daughters, and one large guinea pig. She
likes to read, play racquetball, and play games. You can
learn more about Laura and her writing at her Web site
www.laurasalas.com.

Choose Your Style

Poems explore the entire world, from infinite space to a tiny bug on the sidewalk, from the death of a friend to the silliest way to make a sandwich. No topic is off-limits. And there are as many right ways to write poems as there are poets. Some poets use rhyme, meter, and specific forms to express their thoughts, feelings, and observations. Others write free verse, creating line lengths and shapes on the page that do not fit any preset patterns.

Are you ready to write poetry? Brainstorming and writing activities will help you conquer the blank page. And tips and encouragement from some of today's best poets will help you improve your skills. Whether you want to write poems that make people laugh out loud, gasp in surprise, or see things in a new way, right here is where you begin!

CONTENTS

WANT TO BE A POET?

This book is an excellent way to begin. It will give you plenty of tools and ideas to help you start writing your own poetry. You'll learn how to create startling images and effective shapes on the page, along with satisfying figurative language. Poems and advice from a variety of wonderful poets will help you on your way.

Get the writing habit

Write regularly. Real poets write even on days when they feel bored or unimaginative.

Create a poetry-writing zone.

Keep a journal.

Carry a notebook. Write down how things look and smell and sound. Record funny or sad or fascinating things that happen to you.

Generate ideas

Find an image, real or imagined, that you want to write a poem about. What is the one single thing you want to express about this image?

Brainstorm your topic.

Research your topic. Interesting facts about something can inspire great lines of poetry.

Shut your eyes. Picture your topic in your mind. What do you see?

| GETTING STARTED | POETIC FORMS | LANGUAGE OF POETRY | IMAGERY | POINT OF VIEW |

You can follow your progress by using the bar located on the bottom of each page. The orange color tells you how far along in the poem-writing process you have gotten. As the blocks are filled out, your collection of poems will be growing.

Plan

What is your poem about?

What do you want to compare your topic to?

What mood do you want your poem to have?

What form do you want your poem to take?

Write

Write the first draft, then put it aside for a while.

Does your poem express what you wanted to say?

Condense! Remove unnecessary words.

Does your poem have a good title and a satisfying ending?

Does your poem have surprising words in it?

Publish

Write or print out the final draft.

Keep a copy for yourself.

Send your poem to children's or teen magazines, Internet writing sites, school magazines, or competitions.

METER AND RHYME   POEMS ON THE PAGE   HINTS AND TIPS   THE NEXT STEP

When you get to the end of the bar, your poems are ready to go! You are a poet! Now you can decide how you want to share your poems and what your next project will be. Maybe it will be more poems on the same topic, or maybe something very different.

BEGIN THE POEM

Maybe you think all poets write in quiet, lonely towers, surrounded by English moors. Maybe you think poets have to be serious or boring or heartbroken. Wrong! Poets are just people who look at the world a little bit differently. And they put their version of the world down on paper, in lines instead of in sentences.

What you need

These materials will help you organize your ideas and your findings:

- small notebook that you carry everywhere
- pens, pencils, and highlighters in different colors
- sticky notes to mark ideas in your notebook or to jot down questions
- files and folders to keep poem ideas organized and safe
- camera or sketchpad to record images you don't want to forget
- dictionary, thesaurus, encyclopedia, and rhyming dictionary

Find your writing place

It's nice to have a particular writing place. This place, perhaps your bedroom, is where you almost always write. Set up your rhyming dictionary, your pens, your MP3 player for music, and anything else that makes you feel creative. Tape up pictures that make you think. The pictures might be scenes from nature, pictures of your friends, or funny images someone e-mailed to you. Find a smooth stone or a pair of drumsticks and put them in your writing spot. Sometimes rhythmic motion, like rubbing the stone or tapping the drumsticks, helps your mind run loose.

Follow the writer's golden rule

Once you have chosen your writing space, the first step in becoming a poet is: Go there regularly and write. You must write and write often. This is the writer's golden rule. Until you are sitting at your desk (or in the park or in the doctor's waiting room or at the library) with pen in hand, no writing can happen. It doesn't matter what you write—a description of what's around you, a note to a friend, or a diary entry will do—as long as you write something.

Portable poetry

The great thing about poetry is that it's portable! Having a special writing place is good, but the truth is, you can write poetry anywhere! Because poems are short, you can write a first draft of a poem whenever and wherever it occurs to you. Are you in math class? After you finish your classwork, pop out your notebook and jot down your poem. Walking the dog? Let her sniff around the tree while you park in the grass for a few minutes and write. And all those times you're sitting somewhere, waiting to be picked up or dropped off or joined by a friend—those are prime poetry moments!

GET THE WRITING HABIT

Spies, scientists, and poets have a lot in common. They all observe carefully, ask questions, and record details. Spies are trying to ferret out secrets, and scientists are trying to discover the way the universe works. But poets are usually trying to discover new ways to look at everyday objects and situations. Then they use strong, inventive language to share their discoveries with other people.

Learn the skills

Learning to become a poet can take a long time. You must get used to writing poems regularly, even when you don't feel like it. You might get a great idea in a flash, but it will take steady work to turn your fabulous idea into a terrific poem. Try to write every day. But if you only have two hours free on Saturday mornings, make that your writing time. Just make a commitment to write regularly. Practice writing just as you would a sport or musical instrument.

CASE STUDY

"My childhood interest in rocks turned into straight-up fascination when I learned in ninth grade that the Earth's continents hadn't always looked the way they look now. They had drifted around the planet on huge jigsaw-puzzle plates," says poet Lisa Westberg Peters. "Geologists were showing me a different way of looking at the world and that's exactly why I love poetry: It's a different way of looking at the world. But I still needed years and years of reading and rock-collecting before I could write geology poems with an original and authentic voice."

Now it's your turn

Rough drafts

Throughout this book, you'll be prompted to write rough drafts or try new techniques on existing rough drafts. Don't panic. If you're not sure where to begin, just try one of these methods for getting a rough draft on the page.

- Decide on one thing you want to say about your topic. Write down a phrase about it, and break the phrase into lines.
- Choose a number between five and 10. Write a five-lined poem with that number of syllables on each line.
- Take a poem you like. Copy the first line of it. Now write your own poem that begins with the same first line.
- Take a phrase like "I was" or "My name" or "Dreams are," and write it in five rows on your page. Finish each line with a different phrase.
- Open the dictionary, close your eyes, and point to a word. Write a poem using that word.

Tips and techniques

Brainstorming is the number-one tool for a poet. It's the key that helps you empty out all the weird and wonderful ideas and images that are locked inside your brain. Keep your brainstorming notes in a separate folder or notebook so that you can look back at them later.

Now it's your turn

Brainstorm

Brainstorming exercises are a great way to get words and images flowing. Here's one to try. Open a calendar with pictures to your birthday month and set it on the desk beside you. Sit quietly in your writing place for a few moments. Close your eyes and take four long, deep breaths. Then open your eyes and look at the picture again. Set a timer for two minutes. On a piece of paper, write down as many words that come to mind as you can. They might be obviously related to the picture, or they might not. Don't worry about it. Just write them down. You've found one key to writing. The more you practice like this, the more you will develop your imagination.

FIND YOUR VOICE

What is a poet's voice? It is the unique way a poet puts words together. It is the way you can tell that a certain person wrote a certain poem, even if the poet's name is not given.

Identify the voice

Read a collection of poems by any poet. Then ask yourself, "What did these poems have in common?" Does the poet arrange them on the page similarly? Do many of the poems have the same rhythm? Does the poet write just about nature? The more you read poetry, the more you will begin to recognize other poets' voices.

Finding your writer's voice

The great thing about voice is that you already have one! You don't need to try to find it. Poetry is all about how you see the world around you. So don't try to sound like anyone else when you're writing poetry. Just let the images and words spill onto the paper. Try not to censor yourself. Your poetic voice is a reflection of your personality and thought processes. Reading lots of poetry and writing lots of poetry will help you refine your voice. But you don't need to find it or make it up. You just need to write, and your voice will be on the page.

Now it's your turn

Sound it out

Find a poem that describes an object. It doesn't matter whether you like or don't like the poem. Now close your eyes and picture that object in your mind. What does it look like? Feel like? Sound like? Smell like? What does it remind you of? Write a short poem that describes the same object. Write it in a way that feels natural and feels like you. Now read both poems out loud. How is your poetic voice different from that of the poet who wrote the first poem?

Variety

When you find a poet whose work you like, you might want to only read that writer's poems. But that can be bad for your own writing. You might admire the writer so much that you start imitating his or her style, even if you don't mean to. Read poets you like, of course. But also read lots of anthologies. They are collections of poems by many different poets. That will expose you to various poetic voices and give you a chance to learn from many different writers.

Now it's your turn

Choose a topic for your poem
Look again at your calendar picture from the earlier brainstorming exercise. What does the main item in the picture remind you of? For instance, maybe the picture is of a giraffe. What does the giraffe look like? Maybe it reminds you of a yellow construction crane.

At the top of a blank piece of paper, write, "The _is a_." In this example, you would write, "The giraffe is a construction crane." Now look over the words or phrases you wrote in the previous exercise. Which words might describe both the real item (the giraffe) and the item you're comparing it to (the crane)? List those words under your first line. Don't worry about whether they all make perfect sense. Now you have a word list to draw from for your rough draft.

WRITER'S VOICES

Look at the ways these poets write. How are they different? How are they similar? Which style do you like the best? Which style is closest to your own?

From *Ode to the Sprinkler*
There is no swimming
Pool on
Our street,
Only sprinklers
On lawns,
The helicopter
Of water
Slicing our legs.
We run through
The sprinkler,
Water on our
Lips, water
Dripping
From eyelashes,
Water like
Fat raindrops
That fall from
Skinny trees when
You're not looking.

Gary Soto, from *Neighborhood Odes*

Poem
I loved my friend.
He went away from me.
There's nothing more to say.
The poem ends,
Soft as it began—
I loved my friend.

Langston Hughes, from *The Dream Keeper and Other Poems*

CASE STUDY

"Let your writing bring you happiness," says poet Susan Marie Swanson. "Write about the funny things your little sister does. Write about your favorite tree and the good shade it makes on hot days. Write a letter to your cat."

Michigan Sahara
Sand dunes
in Michigan
are a pretend trip
to the Sahara.

When we empty
the pockets of
our jeans,
out spill
camels,
desert palms,
and scorpions.

Lisa Westberg Peters, from
*Earthshake: Poems from
the Ground Up*

Sorry Back, from the Hamster
I'm sorry I bit your mom's finger
and hung on to it like that.
Hamsters are not normally
bloodthirsty,
but I'd had a lot of adventures by then
and I was tired.
Her hand was a huge scary claw
coming at me.
The blood tasted like rust.

The truth is, at first
I was so, so happy to be free!!!
But later I was so, so glad
to be back
curled in the warm palm
of your hand.

by Ricky
(writing for his hamster)

Joyce Sidman, from *This Is Just to
Say: Poems of Apology and Forgiveness*

Some poems are lines of rhyming text marching straight down the page. But there are many other kinds of poems, too.

A poem can be structured, with a certain number of lines or syllables and a definite rhythm or rhyme. Or it can be the poet's thoughts placed carefully on the page, with no particular pattern followed. Here are different kinds of poems you might like to try.

Free verse

A free verse poem is made of nonrhyming lines that do not follow any certain rhythm, word count, or syllable count. The writer has great freedom in free verse.

Name Dream
Your name lives in a house
with bright windows.
The wind carries your name
with the cottonwood seeds.
Your name clacks
like a smooth stone
knocking against other stones
in the cold waves of the lake.
Your name is a campfire
with tiger shapes in it.

Your name was walking in the night.
There was a long way to walk,
but your name got home.

Susan Marie Swanson, from
Getting Used to the Dark

Tips and techniques
Poets often try out several forms before finding the best one for a particular poem. For instance, if you try to write an acrostic about ALLOWANCE, but you get stuck on the C, you might decide to try a quatrain instead.

Haiku

A haiku contains three lines. The first line has five syllables, the second has seven, and the third has five. This form originated in Japan. It often centers on an image in nature and is set in a particular season. A haiku frequently presents a poetic snapshot of a single, simple moment.

> The spider yo-yos
> down August to a hemlock
> petalworth of shade
>
> J. Patrick Lewis, from
> *Black Swan White Crow*

Acrostic

An acrostic starts with a word written vertically on a page, one letter per line. Each letter is the beginning letter of the first word in a line of the poem. A line might be one word or an entire phrase.

The tiger
Hides in the
Early evening …

Teeth and claws and fur
Invisible hunter
Gold and black stripes hide him
Every inch silently creeping, then suddenly
Roaring, he pounces

Patricia M. Stockland, from *Fur, Fangs, and Footprints: A Collection of Poems About Animals*

Quatrain

A quatrain is a set of four lines, often rhymed. A poem may contain one quatrain or a series of quatrains.

> From *Best Friends*
> It's Susan I talk to, not Tracey,
> Before that I sat next to Jane;
> I used to be best friends with Lynda
> But these days I think she's a pain.
>
> Adrian Henri, from *She's All That! Poems About Girls*

SHAPELY POEMS

A concrete poem takes the shape of its subject. A poem about soccer might be written in the shape of a soccer ball. Or it might even picture a scream!

Write your concrete poems with a pen or pencil. It can be tricky to create concrete poems on the computer, and you might get more caught up with the technical side of things rather than choosing the best words for your poem

BLOODCURDLING SCREAMS

My sister makes this cool noise when she's in the shower and I flush the toilet.

Wait till I get my hands on you, Robert! You did that on purpose.

John Grandits, from *Technically, It's Not My Fault: Concrete Poems*

Cinquain

A cinquain has five lines. Each line has a certain number of syllables.
Line 1: two syllables
Line 2: four syllables
Line 3: six syllables
Line 4: eight syllables
Line 5: two syllables

SweetPea
fluffy
sleeping circle
kisses her paws and purrs,
dreams she's chasing mice and her tail
flickers

Laura Purdie Salas, from
a private collection

Diamante

A diamante poem forms a diamond on the page. Often the nouns in lines 1 and 7 are opposites, or the noun in line 1 transforms into the noun in line 7.
Line 1: a noun
Line 2: two words that describe line 1
Line 3: three "ing" words that describe
    line 1
Line 4: four nouns, two of which describe
    line 1 and two describe line 7;
    or four words that explain the
    relationship between line 1
    and line 7
Line 5: three "ing" words that describe
    line 7
Line 6: two words that describe line 7
Line 7: a noun

summer
bright, yellow
scorching, broiling, growing
opposite seasons, nature's reasons
snowing, swirling, slushing
windy, white
winter

Laura Purdie Salas, from
a private collection

CHAPTER 3: LANGUAGE OF POETRY

Poetry comes in many forms, but one thing that is common throughout all types of poetry is strong language. Poems are short. In order to make an impact, they must contain sparkling, specific words that grab the reader's attention and are fun or interesting to read.

Make it specific

Which is easier to picture: a car or a Volkswagen bug? By using the specific name of something, you help make a picture of that item pop up in your reader's mind. So don't use *flower*, use *sunflower*; don't write *band*, write *Stone Soup*. A specific word carries along some baggage. *Sunflower* makes us think of sunshine and outside, while *roses* carries a romantic feeling. A poem that names Kelly Clarkson in it probably has a different feel than one that names Green Day.

Walk away

Verbs are another area where being specific and concrete helps. Maybe you've used the word *walk* in a rough draft of a poem. It's not that *walk* is a bad word. But we've heard it so many times, we gloss right over it. It doesn't paint a picture in our minds. But any of these words do: *shuffle, scuttle, sneak, tiptoe, dash, stride, strut, mince, scurry, glide,* and *stroll*.

Look at the vivid nouns and verbs in this poem: *fist, silver-mix, raining, tin bouquets, piggyback stars*. These words help your mind picture the jacks being thrown.

Jacks
Tossed
quickly
from an eager fist,
this silver-mix
goes somersaulting,
silver
falling to the walk,
raining
tin bouquets;
small bundles
of piggyback
stars.

Rebecca
Kai Dotlich, from
Lemonade Sun

Assonance and alliteration

Repeated sounds are fun to say. That's one reason we like tongue twisters so much. Assonance is when a vowel sound is repeated over and over. Alliteration is when two or more words begin with the same consonant sound. Using assonance and alliteration makes your poem sound like a poem instead of a paragraph. It's a way to play with words and sounds.

Assonance

Listen to the "ah" sounds in the lines to the right. What mood does the repeated sound give to the poem? Does it have a happy or a melancholy sound? Often the use of repeated "ah" sounds gives a poem a slower, sadder feel.

Alliteration

Listen to the repeated "b," "w," and "r" sounds in this poem.

The belch of a blowfish. The bark of a seal.
The murmuring turn of the tide.
The walloping, wallowing yawn of an eel.
The silence of ships that have died.
Ripples come racing on crystal-blue rollers
With tidings from far and wide.

Kurt Cyrus, from *Hotel Deep: Light Verse from Dark Water*

From *So*
We
climb
another
wobbly
staircase
into
another
hollow
place

Lee Bennett Hopkins, from *Been to Yesterdays: Poems of a Life*

Now it's your turn

Work them in later

Adding some assonance or alliteration is one of the easiest things you can do to revise a poem. First check to see whether you have any repeated sounds. Maybe you already have *belt* and *bracelet*. Then look at the other words in the phrase or line or poem. Can you replace any of these words with words that begin with "b"? Looking up the other words in a thesaurus might help you hit the jackpot.

FIGURATIVE LANGUAGE

With figurative language, you don't say exactly what you mean. Instead, you use metaphors or similes to help the reader see an object in a completely new way.

Metaphors

With a metaphor, you simply call one object another object. A metaphor can be just a small part of a poem, or an entire poem can be one extended metaphor. In his poem *Myrtle,* the poet uses a single metaphor to describe the newspaper carrier, who wears a yellow rain slicker. The poem ends like this:

From my doorway I watch her
flicker from porch to porch as she goes,
a yellow candle flame
no wind or weather dare extinguish.

Ted Kooser, from *Flying at Night: Poems 1965–1985*

This entire poem is one long metaphor. The poet compares the wind to a woman.

The Wind Woman
The Wind's white fingers
Are thin and sharp,
And she plays all night
On an icy harp.

On her icy harp
Of stiff, black trees,
She plays her songs,
And the rivers freeze.

Barbara Juster Esbensen, from *Swing Around the Sun*

Now it's your turn

What is a pencil?

Put a pencil on the table in front of you. Look at the pencil—its shape, color, size, texture. Brainstorm a list of things you can compare to your pencil. If you like, you can write each line like this: "It's as brown (or yellow or black) as a … " Try to come up with at least five comparisons for the pencil. Then write a rough draft of a poem using at least one of the comparisons.

Similes

With a simile, you use *like* or *as* to compare two objects. Similes are sort of the weak cousin of metaphors because the comparison is not quite as strong. Still, a simile can be a fun way to liven up a poem.

What emotion does the poet describe through these similes? Can you feel the narrator's excitement when she compares her mood to a butterfly, a bird's song, or a field of bright red poppies?

From *like sun*
Gran's coming home! Home!
It feels like the first butterfly
or the golden notes of cardinals
or a whole bed of poppies ablaze.

Tracie Vaughn Zimmer, from *Reaching for Sun*

Now it's your turn

Brainstorm

Metaphors and similes don't come easily to everyone. Brainstorming can help. If you want to write about the road in front of your house, for instance, you can ask yourself: What else has the same shape? What else smells like this? What tastes like it? Do people do the same thing to a road that they do to something else? What else has the same texture? What purpose does it serve? What moves like the road? Is the road as gray as something else? Does it twist like an animal? Which one? With questions like these, you might end up comparing the road to a river, sandpaper, a snake, a hallway, the tape on a hospital floor that leads you to the right room, an arrow, a playground, or lots of other things. Then you choose the one that feels closest to what you want to say about the road.

WORDPLAY

Most poets love to play with words. They like the sound of them in their mouths, the way they roll off the tongue. They like double meanings of words. They like to change the spelling of words to see what that does.

You don't have to take poetry too seriously. Have fun with it, and your readers will, too.

Very punny

Puns are a kind of humor in which a word or phrase is twisted a little bit to have a different meaning. For instance, say you were writing a funny poem about a clumsy dog. Maybe you thought of the common phrase, "He has two left feet." But in your poem, since it's a dog, you might say, "He had four left feet." A pun in a poem is a verbal surprise for the reader. It makes the reader stop, smile, and reread. Check out how this poet makes a pun of the word *milkshake*.

> *Shaking*
> Geraldine now, stop shaking that cow
> For heaven's sake, for your sake and the cow's sake.
> That's the dumbest way I've seen
> To make a milk shake.
>
> Shel Silverstein, from *A Light in the Attic*

Funny spellings

Changing the spelling of a word can be great, when it's done on purpose.

> *The Panther*
> The panther is like a leopard,
> Except it hasn't been peppered.
> Should you behold a panther crouch,
> Prepare to say Ouch.
> Better yet, if called by a panther,
> Don't anther.
>
> Ogden Nash, from *Fur, Fangs, and Footprints: A Collection of Poems About Animals*

Onomatopoeia

Snap! Buzz! Hiss! These sound words actually make the sound they describe. That's called onomatopoeia. Using onomatopoeia in your poems makes them fun to read aloud. Listen to how the word *coyote* sounds like a coyote's howl in this poem.

Tips and techniques

It can help to emphasize the word that is onomatopoeic. Don't just write buzz. Write buzzzzzzz. Try hissssss. Or BOOM! Look at some graphic novels or comic books for ideas on how to have fun with sound words. Using invented spelling or font size changes—making whisper smaller than the other words in a line, for instance— emphasizes the word and the sound.

The Coyote
I prowl.
I growl.
My howl
is throaty.
I love
A vowel,
For I am coyo   ote

Douglas Florian, from
*Mammalabilia: Poems
and Paintings*

Now it's your turn

Can you hear it?

Write a rough draft of a poem about a sound you like or hate. Maybe it's your favorite band. Maybe it's robins waking you up at sunrise. Don't worry about wordplay during your rough draft. Just pour out a poem. Now read your rough draft slowly, several times, out loud. Mark spots where you could add sound effects to your poem. Can you replace a word with a sound effect? Try to work in two or three words of onomatopoeia. Read your second draft out loud. Can you hear the difference?

When you write a poem, you want to show the world, not explain it. We each have our own way of looking at the world, and a poem is a way to share your vision. By using sensory details, you can help your reader experience the world the way you do.

Details set the mood. Don't say, "I was sad, and the overcast sky made me sadder." Instead, choose sensory details that support the mood of the poem. Maybe the mood is melancholy. You might describe droopy clouds, or heavy, weighted-down clouds that are as gray as a tombstone. If the mood of your poem is hopeful, you would choose different details or comparisons. You might describe the clouds as giant buckets, ready to pour cleansing water. You might describe the sun peeking out from behind the clouds. What is the mood of Nikki Grimes' poem? Which details give it that mood?

El Noche
I stand out in the cold
el noche and I
both too lonely for whispers.
Only the wind
shatters this silence.
I have been here before
choking in solitude,
but this time
when all the earth
is hollow as a bell,
I hold one end,
ring it,
and you come—
a pale-skinned surprise,
a friend.

Nikki Grimes, from *Bronx Masquerade*

Chart it out

Sometimes it helps to chart your poem. You can make a chart either before you write a first draft or when you are getting ready to revise. Down the left side of a piece of paper, write down things associated with your poem topic. Then fill in as many sense words as you can across the row. You probably won't use all the words you jot down in your poem or revision. But a chart gives you plenty of ideas to work with.

Here's a sample chart for a poem about a basketball game.

Thing	Looks like	Feels like	Smells like	Tastes like	Sounds like
Basketball	leather	shoe sole	chemicals		thunk
	orange		sweat		swish
Sweat	rain on my face	stings eyes	old	salt	
	small rain shower	clings shirt to my back	basement		
	tears	shakes off like a sprinkler	growing things		
Game	a battle	sharp elbow in ribs	popcorn		screech
	scene of panic	hard pass—bowling ball to the chest			whistle

It makes sense(s)

The most effective way to put your view on the page is to use sensory words. They are concrete words that show how something looks, feels, tastes, smells, or sounds. These words make your poem come alive in your reader's mind. Here is an example from poet Ann Turner:

Hieroglyph
A slip, a slide
of feathered toe
and furry leg
that brush the ice
and leave a message
for all to read:
one weasel, here,
before sunup,
dancing in the moonshine
snow

Ann Turner, from *Once Upon Ice and Other Frozen Poems*

When you read a story, you will notice it is told from a particular point of view. The person telling the story, the narrator, controls the flow of information, as well as the way it's presented. A poem can also have a point of view.

First-person poem

This poem has a specific, first-person narrator. It is written from a daughter's point of view, about her father.

No No No
He sits on the couch
staring at me
sitting on the floor
staring anywhere but
back at him.

Homework?

"No."

Hungry?

"No."

Do you want to watch TV?

"No!"

I stand up
to escape to my room.
He catches my hand
as I rush by.

Don't be mad at your mother, Rachel.

I pull my hand away from his,
fast.

"I'm not," I say.
"I'm mad at you."

Susan Taylor Brown, from *Hugging the Rock*

Tips and techniques

First-person poems use the words I or my or me or mine. The narrator is actually in the poem. Most first-person poems share a personal experience. If a poem simply paints a picture, you don't need to be in it. But if you are writing about your relationship with someone else or about something that happened to you, you need to be part of that poem.

Mask poetry

When you write a first-person poem, you don't have to write as you. You can write from the point of view of anybody or anything you want. When you write first-person from the point of view of someone else or something that is not human, or not alive, it is called a mask poem. Here's an excerpt of a poem written from the point of view of a mouse. But it's unlikely the poet is actually a mouse!

The Magical Mouse
I am the magical mouse
I don't eat cheese
I eat sunsets
And the tops of trees
I don't wear fur
I wear funnels
Of lost ships and the weather
That's under dead leaves

Kenneth Patchen, from
*The Collected Poems of
Kenneth Patchen*

Now it's your turn

Imagine
Look outside and choose an item. Maybe it's a tree, a baseball, a squirrel, or even a building. Now shut your eyes and imagine you're that item. What do you feel like? What do you see? What bothers you? Scares you? Write a rough draft of a poem, speaking as that item.

THIRD-PERSON POEMS

In many poems, the narrator is not obvious. You can't tell from the poem who wrote it, and the narrator of the poem is not part of the poem.

Such poems are written from the third-person point of view. The poet does not say *I* or *me* or *mine*. A third-person poem can have people in it. There might be a he or a she or a named person, as in this poem by Gary Soto. But there's no *I* in a third-person poem.

From *Ode to Pablo's Tennis Shoes*
They wait under Pablo's bed,
Rain-beaten, sun-beaten,
A scuff of green
At their tips
From when he fell
In the school yard.
He fell leaping for a football
That sailed his way.
But Pablo fell and got up,
Green on his shoes,
With the football out of reach.

Gary Soto, from *Neighborhood Odes*

Now it's your turn

Tell it twice
Pick a person to write a poem about. Now write two separate rough drafts. In the first rough draft, put yourself in the poem. Write about your relationship with this person and make sure you use I in the poem. In the second draft, keep out of your poem. Do not make yourself a character in it. A reader of the poem should not be able to tell whether the poet has any relationship with the subject of the poem. Which poem do you think works better?

There might not be any people in the poem at all. It might just be an observation of the world, a silly question, or a description. Look at this sample of a third-person poem by Sy Kahn.

Giraffes
Stilted creatures,
Features fashioned as a joke,
Boned and buckled,
Finger painted,

They stand in the field
On long-pronged legs
As if thrust there.
They airily feed,
Slightly swaying,
Like hammer-headed flowers.

Bizarre they are,
Built silent and high,
Ornaments against the sky.
Ears like leaves
To hear the silken
Brushing of the clouds.

Sy Kahn, from *Reflections on a Gift of Watermelon Pickle and Other Modern Verse*

Tips and techniques
If you're writing a poem about someone you know—a teacher, a friend, or someone you love or hate or fear—putting yourself in the poem can make it stronger. It can allow the poem to reveal more about you and the other person. If you want your poem to be less emotional and less personal, try writing it without putting yourself in it. This makes it easier to write more objectively about that person.

CHAPTER 6: METER AND RHYME

Sometimes poetry is like music. It has a strong meter or beat that is made by stressing some words and not others.

Metered poetry often rhymes. Rhyming, metered poetry can be difficult to get right. We'll cover the basics here, but remember that you can write terrific poetry without ever rhyming a single line!

End rhymes

The most popular kind of rhyme is the end rhyme. The last word of one line rhymes with the last word of another line. Here are end-rhyme examples from Jon Scieszka and Shel Silverstein:

Mary Had a ...
Mary had a little worm.
She thought it was a chigger.
But everything that Mary ate,
Only made it bigger.

It came with her to school one day,
And gave the kids a fright,
Especially when the teacher said,
"Now that's a parasite."

Jon Scieszka, from *Science Verse*

Gumeye Ball
There's an eyeball in the gumball machine,
Right there between the red and the green,
Lookin' at me as if to say,
"You don't need any more gum today."

Shel Silverstein, from
A Light in the Attic

Now it's your turn

Give it a try

If you'd like to try writing a metered, rhyming poem, pick out a topic. If you can't think of one, write about a fountain. Come up with a rhythmic first line. End the line with a word that might be pretty easy to rhyme with. Then figure out the rhythm you're using. Now try to write three more lines in that same rhythm. All four lines might rhyme, or you can have two sets of rhyming lines. How did you do?

Rhyme schemes

The rhyme scheme of a poem tells you which lines rhyme with which. Scieszka's poem, for instance, has a rhyme scheme of *abcb defe*. You assign the last word of the first line (*worm*) the letter *a*. Then every end word that rhymes with that word, if there are any, also gets assigned *a*. If the second line does not rhyme with the first line, its last word gets the letter *b*, and all the lines that rhyme with it also get *b*.

Here are verses from three poems and their rhyme schemes:

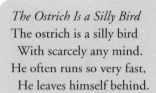

And Stands There Sighing
Down from the north on the north wind flying
the wild geese come: I hear their crying.
Run to the door, and do not mind
that when they are gone, you'll be left behind.
For whoever hears the great flocks crying
longs to be off, and stands there, sighing.

Elizabeth Coatsworth, from *Knock at a Star: A Child's Introduction to Poetry*

Rhyme scheme: *aabbaa*

The Ostrich Is a Silly Bird
The ostrich is a silly bird
  With scarcely any mind.
He often runs so very fast,
  He leaves himself behind.

And when he gets there, has to stand
  And hang about till night,
Without a blessed thing to do
  Until he comes in sight.

Mary E. Wilkins Freeman, from *Knock at a Star: A Child's Introduction to Poetry*

Rhyme scheme: *abcb defe*

The New Colossus: Statue of Liberty Inscription
Give me your tired, your poor,
your huddled masses yearning to breathe free,
the wretched refuse of your teeming shore.
Send these, the homeless, tempest-tossed to me.
I lift my lamp beside the golden door.

Emma Lazarus, from *The Free and the Brave: A Collection of Poems About the United States*

Rhyme scheme: *ababa*

Bad rhyme

Don't commit poetic crimes by forcing tired and offbeat rhymes.

NEAR RHYMES

When two words have similar sounds but don't quite rhyme, it is called near rhyme, or slant rhyme.

Bounce and *house* are near rhymes; so are *shoe* and *few*, and *crash* and *fast*. Here's an example of a near rhyme poem:

Puppy Pileup
Rumble, tumble
bounce bounce bounce
Puppy rampage
Through the house.

Chew a slipper
Drag a shoe
Beg a biscuit
Then a few.

Puppy monster
smash, bang, crash
Puppy pileup
sleeping fast.

by Jan Fields, from a private collection

Internal rhymes

With internal rhyme, one word in a line of poetry rhymes with the last word in that line. Sometimes internal rhyme refers to two words within a line that rhyme, even if one of them is not the last word. Do you hear the internal rhymes in this excerpt from a Robert Graves poem?

Hide and Seek
The trees are tall, but the moon small,
My legs feel rather weak,
For Avis, Mavis and Tom Clarke
Are hiding somewhere in the dark
And it's my turn to seek.

Robert Graves, from *Knock at a Star:
A Child's Introduction to Poetry*

| GETTING STARTED | POETIC FORMS | LANGUAGE OF POETRY | IMAGERY | POINT OF VIEW |

Now it's your turn

Finding rhymes

Use a rhyming dictionary (either in book form or online) to help you find rhymes for a word you're having trouble with. If you don't have access to either one of these, try this. Take the word you want to rhyme. Let's say it's *cheese*. Go through the alphabet in your head and substitute each letter for the beginning sound of your word. So you would say to yourself: aeese, bees, breeze, ceese, deese, fees, fleas, flees, freeze, geese (which looks as if itwould rhyme but doesn't!), heese, etc. As

you go through, write down the ones that actually make words. Then you'll have a list of rhyming words to work from on your poem. Look at a rough draft you would like to make rhyme, and try this technique on at least two words.

Tips and techniques

Rhyming can be tricky, and here's one beginner's mistake to avoid. Don't try to rhyme names! If you write about a girl named Miranda, and suddenly we learn she's a panda, we will all suspect she's only a panda because nothing else rhymes with Miranda. Ditto for hairy Jerry and Jake the snake. Rhyming names? Just don't.

Tips and techniques

Many beginning poets get caught up in trying to rhyme, only to find that rhyming messes up the sound and rhythm of their poem. Remember, poetry does not have to rhyme! If rhyming comes naturally to you, great.

But if your poems start to sound forced or silly or stupid to your own ears, abandon the rhyme. Poetry involves sound, imagery, repetition, form, and so much more. Rhyme is just one small technique that you might or might not want to use.

FEEL THE BEAT

Just as music has rhythm, so does poetry. The meter is the rhythm of your poem.

We define the meter of a poem by identifying the kind of foot it has and how many feet are in each line. Let's look at three common feet in poetry: the iamb, the trochee, and the anapest.

A foot is one unit of a poetic line. Each foot contains one accented syllable (/), plus one or more unaccented syllables (-) in a certain pattern. (// separates syllables)

Name	Syllables	Stress	Examples
Iamb	2	-/	a **sin**//gle **pat**//tern **in**
Trochee	2	/-	**I** don't//**need** a//**milk** bowl
Anapest	3	--/	In this **wild**//no-man's **sha**//dow where **hea**//vy winds **rolled**

How many feet in a line?

We also identify poems by how many feet are in each line. If you have an iambic poem—that is, you have written it in iambs—you might have five iambs in each line. That would be iambic pentameter (*penta* for five).

There is a different name for each line, depending on how many feet it has.

1	monometer
2	dimeter
3	trimeter
4	tetrameter
5	pentameter
6	hexameter
7	heptameter
8	octameter

Iambs

To the right are five lines written in iambs. Can you name the type of each line?

Excerpt from *409* (*The Battle-Field*)
They dropped like Flakes–
They dropped like Stars–
Like Petals from a Rose–
When suddenly across the June–
A wind with fingers–goes–

Emily Dickinson, from *The Complete Poems of Emily Dickinson*

(iambic dimeter, iambic dimeter, iambic trimeter, iambic tetrameter, iambic trimeter)

Now it's your turn

Start at the end

Writing metered poetry can be really difficult. Sometimes you read your own poem, and it flows perfectly. That might be because you wrote it, so you know just how you want it to sound. But then when a friend or a teacher or your sister reads it, that person stumbles all over the words. Here's a tip. Read your poem out loud, slowly, one line at a time. But start with the last line and work your way up. Read the line as if you're having a conversation. Ignore the rhythm you know it's *supposed* to have. What rhythm comes out naturally? Put an accent mark over the syllables you stress as you read it. Once you reach the top line, look at your marks. Can you see a pattern? More important, can you see where the pattern is broken? That's the part of the poem you need to revise.

Trochees

Here's the opening line from *The Raven*, a famous poem by Edgar Allan Poe. Do you hear the pounding beat of the trochees? Can you name this type of line?

> Once upon a midnight dreary, while I pondered, weak and weary,
>
> (trochaic octameter)

Anapests

Here are two lines written in anapests. Can you name the type of each line?

> If I go, if I go, and I never come back
> Will you wish for me now and again?
>
> Laura Purdie Salas, from a private collection
>
> (anapestic tetrameter, anapestic trimeter)

UNRHYMED OR UNMETERED POETRY

Beginning poets often feel drawn to writing metered, rhyming poems, but they are harder than you might think.

You might get so caught up in trying to get the right rhythm and rhyme that you forget to express your thoughts, your observations, or your sense of humor. Make sure to explore writing in unrhymed or unmetered form as well.

Tips and techniques

Piggybacking on another poet can make it easier to practice meter. Some people find it simpler to get started by taking theme songs from television shows or just songs from the radio. They choose songs that rhyme and have strong beats. Then they write poems about completely different subjects, using the same rhyme schemes and meters as the original songs.

Blank verse

Blank verse does not rhyme, but it does have a meter. It is written in iambic pentameter. Many of William Shakespeare's plays were written in blank verse.

Here is an example of blank verse from Shakespeare's *Romeo and Juliet*.

> But soft! What light through yonder window breaks?
> It is the East, and Juliet is the sun!
> Arise, fair sun, and kill the envious moon
> Who is already sick and pale with grief
>
> From *Romeo and Juliet*, Act II, Scene 1,
> by William Shakespeare

Now it's your turn

Try a few

What's a topic you'd like to explore? Making a touchdown, doing your homework, playing catch with your golden retriever? Choose one topic and write four rough drafts. Use a different form for each poem. Write two poems using meter and rhyme. And write two poems that do not rhyme and are not metered. Remember, these are only first drafts! Just follow the rules of the form and see what words come to you. Which form do you think works best for your chosen topic? How different are your poems?

Free verse

Although blank verse is not blank, free verse is definitely free. Poems written in free verse do not follow any particular rhythm. They still sound like poetry, however, because they make good use of repetition of words and phrases. If a poem is not blank verse, rhymed verse, or a special form like a haiku or cinquain, then it's probably free verse. This is the most open-ended option for poetry writing.

Here is an example of free verse from poet Kathi Appelt.

From *Homecoming*
Normally, he hates being the shortest boy
in the tenth grade
shorter even than
most of the girls;

normally, short is a problem
to be such a shrimp
pee-wee
short stuff;

but tonight's not normal
tonight he's dancing with Laticia Sanders
the tallest girl
in the tenth grade;

Kathi Appelt, from *Poems from Homeroom: A Writer's Place to Start*

TAKE OUT

Condensation is key to most good poetry. No, not the drops of water that form outside your water glass. In poetry, we're talking about condensing information, using the fewest words possible.

Maybe you are writing a poem about sunset and the end of the day. Once you have a rough draft of the poem, try cutting it in half. Get rid of all these words: *a, an, the.* How does it sound? Have you used two words when one would do? Does each word and line add needed information to your poem? Making your poems compact and filled with great words takes lots of practice.

Narrow your options

Free verse gives you lots of options as a poet. Sometimes it can feel like too many, and you don't know where to start. There are plenty of ways to give yourself a structure to work within, at least at the beginning. You might find as the poem develops that you abandon the structure, and that's fine. Sometimes you can use it just as a stepstool to reach the next level of your poem. Choose a topic, and try one of these three methods to write a rough draft right now.

- Write a short phrase about your topic. Now write it at the top and bottom of a blank page, as well as right in the middle. Write your poem and use that phrase as the opening and closing lines and as a refrain in the middle.

- Roll a die. Write a free verse poem with that many syllables in each line.

- Write down your 10-digit phone number. Now write a poem based on that number in this way: Each digit indicates the number of words in one line of poetry. So if your number is 488-555-2145, your poem's first line would have four words, the second line eight words, etc. For a 0, either skip that line or use 10 words.

Repeat, repeat, repeat

Repetition is an important technique in many kinds of poetry. Free verse uses it a lot. Repetition of words and phrases can help emphasize an important idea. It can also give the poem a more musical sound.

Read these three samples of poems using repetition. What do you think the poet accomplishes by repeating words or phrases? Does the repetition let the poet emphasize a particular word or idea? Does it make the poem more fun to read aloud?

Into the Mud
Sun
slants low,
chill seeps into black
water. No more days of bugs
and basking. Last breath, last sight
of light and down I go, into the mud. Every
year, here, I sink and settle, shuttered like a
shed. Inside, my eyes close, my heart slows
to its winter rhythm. Goodbye, goodbye! Remember the warmth.
Remember the quickness.
Remember me.
Remember.

Joyce Sidman, from *Song of the Water Boatman and Other Pond Poems*

This Is My Rock
This is my rock,
And here I run
To steal the secret of the sun;

This is my rock,
And here come I
Before the night has swept the sky;

This is my rock,
This is the place
I meet the evening face to face.

David McCord, from *Every Time I Climb a Tree*

Primer Lesson
Look out how you use proud words.
When you let proud words go, it is
     not easy to call them back.
They wear long boots, hard boots; they
     walk off proud; they can't hear you
     calling—
Look out how you use proud words.

Carl Sandburg, from *Rainbows Are Made: Poems by Carl Sandburg*

A poem looks very different on the page from a short story or a novel. Poems are written in lines, not paragraphs.

Poems can be written in phrases and strings of words, not necessarily sentences. As the poet, you have the freedom to arrange the words on the page however you think works best for the content of your poem.

Line breaks

One of the most important decisions you make as a poet is where to end each line. Some poets end their lines where they want the reader to insert a very small pause. Many poets break their lines at the end of a phrase.

Another thing to consider is the weight of the line. Each line in a poem carries about the same weight. So if you have a word that is really important to your poem, you might want it to stand alone as a line.

Poet Dorothy Aldis could have made the last two lines of *When I Was Lost* into one line. Why do you think she broke it into two? What effect does that have on how you read the lines and on how important they seem? Does the pause between the last two lines give the words *hollow* and *alone* more weight?

When I Was Lost
Underneath my belt
My stomach was a stone.
Sinking was the way I felt.
And hollow.
And alone.

Dorothy Aldis, from *All Together: A Child's Treasury of Verse*

In the poem, *In the Bathtub of Possibilities*, a child is pretending to be different things while taking a bath. Kelly R. Fineman puts each role on its own line: a landscaper, an admiral, a mermaid, Alice. Each new short line signals to the reader that now the poet is talking about this different role. It also makes clear that the line or lines that follow are describing what the child is doing in that specific role.

In the Bathtub of Possibilities

I am:

    a landscaper
        clearing a lake amid bubble mountains

    an admiral
        directing battles between rubber ducks
        and drakes

    a mermaid
        my hair a floating halo
        or fishnet

   Now, Alice
      in a towel
          too big for the rabbit-hole drain

   Kelly R. Fineman, from a private collection

Tips and techniques

One way to think about the weight of each line is in terms of money. Imagine that you need to make each line in your poem worth one dollar. Think of tiny, unimportant words, such as *a* and *the*, as nickel words. Verbs and nouns are worth more—perhaps a quarter. And then there's the most important word in your poem, the surprising word that is crucial to what your poem means. That one word might be a dollar all by itself. This isn't an exact or

mathematical equation, of course. It's just a way to think about your words and how many you might want to have in any single line.

END-STOPPED VS. ENJAMBED LINES

If a line ends with a strong pause, at the definite end of a thought, it is called an end-stopped line.

Sometimes a poet will use a period or other punctuation for an end-stopped line. An enjambed line is the opposite of an end-stopped line. Now one thought runs over from one line to the next.

Here's an example of an end-stopped rhyme. Read it out loud and listen to how almost every line ends with your voice going down.

From *The Dog*
Asleep he wheezes at his ease.
He only wakes to scratch his fleas.

He hogs the fire, he bakes his head
As if it were a loaf of bread.

He's just a sack of snoring dog.
You can lug him like a log.

You can roll him with your foot,
He'll stay snoring where he's put.

Ted Hughes, from *The Cat and the Cuckoo*

Here's a poem with enjambed lines. Listen to how smoothly one line flows into the next.

Child Frightened by a Thunderstorm
Thunder has nested in the grass all night
and rumpled it, and with its outstretched wings
has crushed the peonies. Its beak was bright,
sharper than garden shears and, clattering,
it snipped bouquets of branches for its bed.
I could not sleep. The thunder's eyes were red.

Ted Kooser, from *Official Entry Blank*

Give it a break

Here are the words to the poem *Elephant* by Valerie Worth. The words appear in paragraph style, but the poet actually wrote them in lines. Write this poem down and break it into lines in the way that you think works best.

The elephant consents to curl her trunk on command, to stand on a tub, and other foolish tricks that are part of her job; but when it is time for the tent to move to another town, she is the only one who can pull the tall poles down.

See page 45 for the poem as written by the poet.

Tips and techniques

If you're having trouble breaking your poem into lines, write two or three versions of the poem—same words, but different line breaks. Now give your versions to a few friends to read out loud. Listen carefully to where they pause. Which words do they emphasize? Do they read the lines slowly or quickly? Paying attention to how readers interpret line breaks will help you decide the best places to end your lines.

THE SHAPE OF YOUR POEM

You can put your poem down the left margin of the page, center it, or slide it down the right side. You can write your poem vertically, horizontally, or in some combination of both.

You might make some words **bold**, *italicized*, or ALL CAPITAL LETTERS. You might place bigger   spaces   between some words to indicate a longer pause or a jumpy rhythm. Basically, you can arrange your poem on the page however you want.

Here are three poems arranged by their authors. Which do you like? Read the poems out loud. How does the shape of the poem affect how you read it?

When I Grow Up
I want to be an artist, Grandpa—
write and paint, dance and sing.

                    Be accountant.
                    Be lawyer.
                    Make good living,
                    buy good food.
                    Back in China,
                    in the old days,
                    everybody
                    so, so poor.
                    Eat one chicken,
                    work all year.

Grandpa, things are different
here.

Janet S. Wong, from *A Suitcase of Seaweed and Other Poems*

Doors
An open door says, "Come in."
A shut door says, "Who are you?"
Shadows and ghosts go through shut doors.
If a door is shut and you want it shut,
     why open it?
If a door is open and you want it open,
     why shut it?
Doors forget but only doors know what it is
     doors forget.

Carl Sandburg, from *Rainbows Are Made:
Poems by Carl Sandburg*

Now it's your turn

Shapely

Choose a new topic or pick a rough draft you've written before. Then revise your poem, using any other shape besides just lines marching down the left margin. But to view lines on the march, here is the published version of Valerie Worth's *Elephant* poem from page 43. Does it look like you thought it would?

Elephant
The elephant
Consents to curl
Her trunk on
Command, to stand
On a tub,
And other foolish
Tricks that are
Part of her job;

But when it is time
For the tent
To move to another
Town, she
Is the only one
Who can pull
The tall
Poles down.

Valerie Worth, from *Animal Poems*

Beat Writer's Block

When you can't think of a single thing to write, that's writer's block. It's frustrating, irritating, and enough to make you feel as if you're not a writer.

The main cause of writer's block is the monster that sits on your shoulder as you write. It's an ugly little beast called your internal critic. While you write, it whispers in your ear: "That stinks. You call that a poem? Rubbish."

Kick out the critic

Silencing your internal critic takes work. When you find yourself criticizing your writing, brush off your shoulder. Write a poem about the critic and what you'd like to do to it! Brainstorm a list of 10 poem topics you'd like to write about. Take an existing poem you like and write your own version of it, changing the words to make it a spoof or funny version.

A complete blank

Sometimes you look at the blank page and you have no idea what to write about. Here are three things to try.

- Find a published poem you don't like. Then write a poem you *do* like about the same topic.
- Listen to a song you like. Now write a poem that "answers" the song.
- Find a magazine or newspaper article that interests you. Write a poem using individual words and phrases from the article.

Tips and techniques

Poems can take some time to grow. Trying to force a particular poem usually doesn't work. You want the poem to flow out of you. If you have to drag it out, kicking and screaming, the poem likely won't be very good. So if one poem doesn't work, try another one. Don't feel bad about abandoning a poem for a while until it feels as if it's ready to come to life.

Consider feedback

Your internal critic must be silenced while you're working on your first draft. For a first draft, you need to be free to write whatever comes out of your head and onto the page. But once you've revised a poem and made it as magical as you can, it's helpful to have other people read it. Ask your friends or teachers to read your poems, out loud, and give you some feedback. Ask them what works well and what doesn't. Try not to take it personally. They're talking about your poem, not about you as a person! It can be tough to listen to someone point out problems with your work. But listen closely (and be polite). Considering other people's ideas can help you really make your work sparkle.

CASE STUDY

How does a poet stay inspired and keep coming up with new ideas?

"I suppose my curiosity would be the good culprit," says poet Rebecca Kai Dotlich. "Always wanting to know that unknown or clouded fact, that small or hidden detail. And, always, reading books."

Now it's your turn

Get going again

Sometimes you start off a poem with great enthusiasm, but then you lose steam halfway through and can't figure out where to go next. If your poem stalls, try the "What if" exercise. Read your poem out loud. Then ask yourself:

- What if the poem goes in a completely unexpected direction right now?
- What if I try a different form for this poem? (Haiku or concrete?)
- What if I give this poem a surprise ending?
- What if a friend were writing this poem? How might he or she approach it?
- What if I felt the opposite way about the subject of this poem?

If none of this helps, maybe it's time to work on a different poem for a while.

LEARN THE TRICKS OF THE TRADE

To be a poet, it helps to constantly fill the well of your imagination. Here are some good habits that will help make you a better poet.

Do something else!

Leaving your writing place, especially if you're blocked, really helps. Go for a walk, take a shower, go to a science or art museum. Learn about a topic you know nothing about. All of these activities can help both empty and fill your mind. Empty it of stress and pressure; fill it with new ideas, new details, new poems.

Keep a journal

Many writers find it helpful to keep a daily journal. You can write about your family, your friends, what happens at school, how your sports teams are doing, or whatever else you feel like. You can write lists, paragraphs, or even poems. One fun exercise is to write a short poem every day. Give yourself a word limit. Maybe each poem is 20 words or fewer. That will take the pressure off. Each day just describe one item in a short poem. This kind of daily writing will help keep your poetry muscles strong.

Take or make pictures

Take a camera or a sketchpad and explore outside or around your town. Take photographs or draw pictures to show the details of things that catch your eye. Don't think about the words you would use to describe them. Just try to capture objects visually. Let your mind soak up the patterns, colors, and textures around you, and give the language part of your brain a rest for a while.

CASE STUDY

"I write every single day," says poet Tracie Vaughn Zimmer. "Not always poetry but something—e-mail, blogs, letters, grocery lists, ideas, descriptions, title lists, character sketches, facts I heard on the radio, something I need to Google. They feed my current project but also give me hope that another idea will soon be kindled from this tinder of words."

Get wet

Go jump in a lake! Or the ocean or a swimming pool. Or even just take a shower or soak in a bathtub. Many writers and other kinds of artists say they get some of their best ideas while in water. The next time you're all wet, float, soak, or stand there and empty your mind. See what pictures or thoughts come into your head. Your next poem topic may be just a water drop away.

Take notes

Listening to music is a great way to recharge your creative batteries. Put on some tunes of any kind—rock, jazz, classical, hip-hop, country—and pay attention to how the music affects you. Listen to the lyrics and think about what makes a great song. Consider how different musical sounds, rhythms, and speeds affect your own moods. Or just lie back and let waves of sound roll over you. Sometimes *not* thinking too hard is exactly the break your brain needs.

Open your eyes

The basis of much great poetry is simply observation. Poems are all about sharing how you see the world. And to do that, you actually have to *see* the world. Look around you. Listen. Watch how nature works. Watch how people interact with each other.

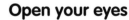

Now What?

By now you probably have at least a handful of poems written. Congratulations! Poems are short, but that doesn't mean they're easy. By putting your vision of the world onto the page, you have shared a part of yourself. So where do you go from here?

Pick your favorites

You've already looked at your individual poems for possible revision. But now just spread out your poems and read through them. Which ones do you enjoy the most? Which are you the most proud of? Do any make you smile or laugh? Do any make your stomach hurt with their harsh reality? Set aside your favorite poems.

Pick a project

Now look at your favorite poems. What do they have in common? Maybe you have a flair for writing rhymed, funny poems. Or have you fallen in love with haiku? What topics seem to draw the most powerful poems from you?

Poems work well in collections, because they usually have more impact when they're grouped together. If you like a specific form, like acrostics or cinquains, a collection of poems in that form might be a great project for you. If you choose one form, you still might want to narrow your topic. Maybe you want to write a collection of cinquains about your experiences at school or as a figure skater or football player. Or you might want to put together a collection of acrostics about all sorts of subjects and in a variety of moods.

Perhaps one topic fascinates you. Maybe you love swimming or basketball or the zoo near your house. You could write a collection exploring this topic. Different poems could show the funny, the scary, and the twisted side of your topic. You could explore this one topic through all kinds of poems: rhyming, free verse, haiku, diamante, and more.

Aim for about 15 poems in your collection. That's enough to really get into a topic or a form. But it's not an overwhelming number to shoot for. Obviously if you really get into it and you end up writing 40 poems, that's terrific! Don't stop yourself if you have a poetic flow going.

You can try a couple of techniques while working on your collection. Many poets find it easiest to write a whole collection's worth of rough drafts and then go back and revise them all. Other people like to write a poem, revise it, polish it, and *then* move on to the next poem. The trick is to do what feels right to you. After you finish a first draft of a poem, do you feel an urge to work on it right away? Or are you eager to move on to your next idea, your next poem?

A collection of collections

Here are some examples of the kinds of collections poets have put together and published.

Marvelous Math, compiled by Lee Bennett Hopkins, contains poems about your favorite subject!

Science Verse, by Jon Scieszka, features science-based spoofs on classic poems.

She's All That! Poems About Girls, compiled by Belinda Hollyer, has poems—from sassy to serious—all about girls.

The World According to Dog: Poems and Teen Voices, by Joyce Sidman, features poems about dogs, accompanied by brief essays written by teens about their own dogs.

When Riddles Come Rumbling: Poems to Ponder, by Rebecca Kai Dotlich, features riddles in the form of poems.

WHEN A COLLECTION WON'T COME

As with any poetry project, forcing
it doesn't work very well.

Maybe you're working
on a collection
of diamantes
about the
four seasons or
quatrains about
mythical creatures. But
you're not feeling very inspired on that
topic today, even after brainstorming. That's OK. Take a break
and work on something completely unrelated to that project.
The next day, try going back to your original project.

CASE STUDIES

"Poems you write must come from within your heart …
not your pen nor head, not even your imagination … from
your heart," says poet Lee Bennett Hopkins.

"Whenever I'm stuck on a poem I remind myself to focus
on my senses," says poet Tracie Vaughn Zimmer. "The
sense of smell and finding that Just Right sound can make a
poem suddenly wake up when it was asleep on the page."

When your collection is done

After you finish a set of poems that will make up your collection, set
them aside. Your brain needs a break from them. You can work on titles
for your collection and can certainly start writing new poems or a new
collection. But try to put aside this collection for at least two weeks.

Think of a title

Once you have a collection completed and you've set it aside for awhile
(which you should always do!), start thinking about a title. A fun,
appealing title will draw people into your poems. Try to reflect the
mood of your poems. You don't want a serious title on a collection of
silly poems. Then your readers won't get what they expect.

Check out some titles

Here are a few effective poetry titles. Which ones do you like best? What do you think makes them effective? Do they make you laugh? Do they make you wonder what the poem or book is about? Do they have words in unexpected combinations?

Astronaut Stopping by a Planet on a Snowy Evening (from *Science Verse* by Jon Scieszka)
The Flaming Lake (from *Moving Day* by Ralph Fletcher)
The Great Beyond (from *Comets, Stars, the Moon, and Mars* by Douglas Florian)
Instructions for the Earth's Dishwasher (from *Earthshake: Poems from the Ground Up* by Lisa Westberg Peters)
The Moth's Serenade (from *Joyful Noise Poems for Two Voices* by Paul Fleischman)

Now it's your turn

Titles from A to Z

Take a piece of paper and write the alphabet down the left side of the page. Now set a timer for five minutes. As fast as you can, try to write a title that starts with each letter of the alphabet. Don't edit yourself, and don't listen to your internal critic saying that a title is stupid. Just write as fast as you can. Many of your titles will sound similar, since the same words might appear in a lot of them. That's OK. Just try to fill out one title beginning with each letter. Q, X, and Z might be especially tough. If you can't think of a title for one, just move on to the next letter. Keep writing until the timer goes off or until you have a title for every letter, whichever is first. Then read your list aloud and see whether you've written a winner of a title!

Ask Giraffe about the Rainbow
Bananas Grow upside down
Cat Who Licked the moon
Dogs don't smell daffodils
East Wind Blows West
Frightened by the Thunderstorm
Giraffes Can Reach the Clouds
Hush! Do You Hear the Thunder?
I've made A Wish Upon a Shooting Star
J
Kissed by the Shooting stars
L
Moon Caught in the Ripples
N
Once Upon a Rainbow
Poems About Animals and Nature
Q
Rainbow Rhymes
Secrets of the Silent Rain

LEARN FROM THE POETS

Teens don't often get the chance to speak with poets, so here a few poets give you their best tips.

Susan Marie Swanson

Susan Marie Swanson (above) published her very first poem when she was 10 years old. Her poem about snowflakes was published in her small Illinois town's weekly newspaper. Today she is an award-winning poet, and her books include *Getting Used to the Dark*, a collection of poems, and *To Be Like the Sun*, a picture book. "The thing that has helped me most in my writing," she says, "is learning that a poem often begins with a few clumsy words. It helps to start small—not with the whole bike but with the silver gleam of the handlebars, not with the whole dog but with the way he turns in circles before he lies down on the kitchen rug."

Rebecca Kai Dotlich

Rebecca Kai Dotlich started keeping a diary when she was 11. She made lists of her favorite words and copied favorite poems into it. Today she is the author of many poetry collections and has won awards for her work. "Don't try too hard to write in forms; your poetry might fall onto the page somewhat forced," she says. "Try, instead, to write down first what you feel, what you see, what you are curious about, or even what you are doing. Just write it down. Then go back and see how you can make your thoughts, lines and words more poetic. An example might be:

"1st): That frog is jumping from rock to rock and looks silly.

"2nd): That silly frog,
all strong and green,
jumps on rocks
like a jumping bean.

"Or, if you don't want it to rhyme, don't!

"3rd): That silly frog,
all strong and green,
jumps from rock to rock,
croaking proud songs
to pond and sky."

Tracie Vaughn Zimmer

Tracie Vaughn Zimmer began keeping a journal in fifth grade and filled it "with really embarrassing stuff." She began writing for publication as an adult, and her first book, *Sketches from a Spy Tree*, is a series of poems from an 11-year-old girl's point of view. Her second book, *Reaching for Sun*, is also a story told through poems. "If you read 100 books of poetry (old, new, contemporary, traditional, etc.) no one will have to teach you anything about poetry," she says. "You will have ingested everything you ever need to know."

Lee Bennett Hopkins

Lee Bennett Hopkins grew up in poverty in the projects of Newark, New Jersey. As an adult, he turned his childhood memories into an auto-biographical collection called *Been to Yesterdays: Poems of a Life*. "If you want to write poetry," he says, "rewrite your work. I often feel there is no such thing as writing … ONLY … rewriting!" Hopkins is an award-winning poet, though he is perhaps even more well-known for his anthologies. He puts together collections of poems by diverse poets to create wonderful, subject- or form-themed anthologies like *Marvelous Math* and *Wonderful Words: Poems About Reading, Writing, Speaking, and Listening!*

Joyce Sidman

Joyce Sidman (right) has been writing since grade school. She has always felt compelled to write, and she discovered poetry in high school. She says the sleekness of poetry—the lack of extra words—attracts her. She writes mostly about nature and animals, and her award-winning collections include *Song of the Water Boatman and Other Pond Poems* and *Butterfly Eyes and Other Secrets of the Meadow*. "I find that the more I write, the more brainstorming and prewriting I do in my head, rather than on paper," she says. "As I take my daily walks or stare out the window, I am picking up ideas, words and phrases and looking at them with a critical eye: Will this work? Will this? By the time I start writing, the poem is already half alive."

Why do poets write?

- To share their vision of the world
- To feel relief when they empty out their minds
- To make people laugh
- Because they have to

PREPARE YOUR WORK

After you've let your poems sit in a desk drawer for a while, take them out and read them fresh. With the time away, you'll be able to look at them more objectively now and see where they need more work.

Revise your poems

Read each poem aloud, slowly, two times. Then go through it with a pen and work on these questions. Is it condensed? Get rid of every extra word. Your poem should be as short as it can be, whether that is 15 words or 85 words. Use the smallest number of words possible to say what you need to say. Make your nouns and verbs specific and concrete. Is the shape or form of the poem on the page the strongest it can be? Have you used word placement and line breaks to tell the reader where to stop or pause, or perhaps to surprise the reader?

Look for ways to add figurative language, such as alliteration, assonance, or onomatopoeia, to your poem. Have you used any similes or metaphors? You don't need to use all of these in every poem, of course, but a sprinkling of various poetic devices should appear in most poems. It's part of what makes them poems, not paragraphs.

A helping voice

If you've written rhyming poems, ask someone else to read them aloud, twice, slowly. Listen to where the reader stumbles. Check your beats, your rhythm. Are they consistent? Or are you expecting your reader to stress certain syllables that wouldn't usually be stressed just to keep the right rhythm?

Try out your titles

Read your collection title and your poem titles out loud. Which ones are most intriguing? Which is your favorite? Can you work on your other titles to try to make them as good as your favorite one?

Book it

If you have a computer at your home, school, or library, you can use it to print your poetry collection. Choose the fonts (type styles) that you like and arrange your poems on the pages. Place each poem on a separate page. You can decide where on the page it should be. Down the left margin, centered, some other place? You can also change the order of your poems. If you have a mix of silly and serious poems, it's often good to group your poems together within your collection. You might want all your nature poems together and then all your school poems. Or group all your silly poems, then move on to your more serious poems. Once you're happy with your collection, print it.

Create a cover

You can also create your cover on the computer. Use a graphics program to scan and print art that you create, or download copyright-free (meaning it's OK to use) clip art. Play with images and your title until you have the cover just the way you want it. Don't forget to include your name as the author! Then print your cover. Now you can place your collection and cover in a slim binder or report cover to protect your work.

CASE STUDIES

"The single most important revision technique I use in poetry is reading my work out loud (to myself, or maybe to my dog)," writes Joyce Sidman. "Poetry should sing, even if it doesn't rhyme. Whatever sounds awkward, slow, or dull needs to be cut out or pepped up with vivid language."

Rebecca Kai Dotlich says, "I write on the computer and love to cut and paste, switch lines around, 'try on' different words. I usually print out my revisions and tape them up on the wall, referring to them as I write my final draft."

REACH YOUR AUDIENCE

You've completed a poetry collection. Excellent! Now you can find people who will be your audience, your readers. You might want your audience to include your family and friends and maybe even strangers.

Places to publish your poems

There are a few magazines and some writing Web sites that accept poems from young writers. Each magazine and Web site has its own rules about how to submit your work, so make sure you follow the directions. Because poems are short and quick to read, you have more options for getting your work before the public. Here are some other ways you can present your work. Some will reach just a few people, and others could reach many people. The key is sharing your work with others.

- Submit poems to your school's newspaper or literary magazine.
- Offer to share a poem on a bulletin board in a classroom.
- Post a poem on the outside of your locker, if this is allowed.
- If you have a personal Web page or space, post your poems there.
- Hold a poetry slam at lunch or in your English class. That's where you perform poems in a dramatic, powerful, or funny way.
- Put up a new poem on your family's refrigerator every week.

Poetry clubs

It can be fun to share your work with others through a poetry club. You could recite your poems and learn how to critique each other's works. This will help you improve your poetry skills. Your club could also hold poetry slams and perhaps put out a poetry magazine. Check with your school, library, or bookstore about providing a meeting space.

Finding a publisher

If you submit some poems to magazines, make sure to read their guidelines and follow them. In general, you should not send more than five poems at a time, and each poem should be on a separate page. Put your name and contact information on each page. Send a short cover letter that describes what you're sending, and include a self-addressed, stamped envelope for them to return your poems.

Study writers' guidebooks for the names of magazines that publish the work of young poets. Anything you submit to a publisher should be typed, not handwritten. And keep in mind that the competition is fierce. Most submissions do *not* get published. But if you're serious about your poems, it can't hurt to start submitting now. It can keep you motivated for writing new poems.

Rejection

Try not to take rejections personally. Professional, published writers get rejected all the time! It's just part of the process. Keep in mind there are many reasons work gets rejected, and not all the reasons mean the poem itself is bad. It's bold and exciting to submit your work for publication, but there are lots of other ways to share your work with others.

Some final words

Poems can accomplish so many things. They can make people laugh or cry. They can make people think about something they've never thought about before. And they can entertain both you, while you're writing them, and your readers, while they're reading them. Poetry is an endless discovery about yourself and the world around you.

Read! Write! Observe!

And keep surprising yourself and other people by turning the world into poems.

Glossary

acrostic—a poem form in which the first letters of all lines form a word when read vertically down the page

alliteration—when several words begin with the same consonant sound

anapest—a three-syllable poetry foot with the rhythm - - /

anthologies—collections of poems by various poets

assonance—the repetition of a vowel sound

blank verse—unrhymed lines of iambic pentameter

cinquain—a five-line poem with a certain number of syllables in each line

concrete poem—a poem written in the shape of its subject

condense—to get rid of unnecessary words

critique—to give feedback about what works well or not so well in a piece of writing

diamante—a poem written in a diamond shape on the page

end rhyme—lines of a poem with last words that rhyme

end-stopped—a line that breaks at the end of a complete thought

enjambed—a line that breaks in the middle of a thought

extended metaphor—an entire poem that is a comparison of two items

figurative language—language that says one thing but means another; metaphors and similes are examples of figurative language

first-person viewpoint—a viewpoint that has a single character reciting the poem as if he or she had written it; readers feel as if that character is talking directly to them

free verse—unrhymed, unmetered poetry

haiku—a Japanese poetry form that usually has 17 syllables, or beats, in three lines (five syllables in the first and last lines and seven in the middle)

iamb—a two-syllable foot of poetry with the meter - /

internal rhyme—when a word inside a line rhymes with the last word in the line

line break—where a line ends

mask poem—a first-person poem written from the point of view of someone other than the poet or an animal or even an object that is not living

metaphor—a figure of speech that paints a word picture; calling a man "a mouse" is a metaphor from which we learn in one word that the man is timid or weak, not that he is actually a mouse

meter—the rhythm of a poem

near rhyme—when two words have similar sounds but do not actually rhyme

onomatopoeia—sound words that make the sound they describe, such as *buzz*

poetry slam—when people dramatically perform poems they have written

point of view—the eyes through which a poem is told

quatrain—a poem or verse written in four-line sections

revise—to write a new, improved version of a poem

rhyme scheme—a set of letters that tells which lines rhyme with others in a poem

simile—saying something is like something else, a word picture, such as "clouds like frayed lace"

third-person viewpoint—a viewpoint that has someone outside the poem describe the events in that poem

trochee—a two-syllable poetry foot with the meter / -

Permissions and Acknowledgements

"Ode to the Sprinkler," 12. From *Neighborhood Odes*, copyright © 1992 by Gary Soto, illustrations copyright © 1992 by David Diaz, reprinted by permission of Harcourt, Inc. "Poem," 12. From *The Dream Keeper and Other Poems* by Langston Hughes, copyright © 1994 by the Estate of Langston Hughes. Used by permission of Alfred A. Knopf, a division of Random House, Inc. "Michigan Sahara," 13. From *Earthshake: Poems from the Ground Up*, copyright © 2003 by Lisa Westberg Peters. Used by permission of the author. "Sorry Back, from the Hamster," 13. *This Is Just To Say: Poems of Apology and Forgiveness* by Joyce Sidman. Text copyright © 2007 by Joyce Sidman. Reprinted by permission of Houghton Mifflin Company. All rights reserved. "Name Dream," 14. From *Getting Used to the Dark*, copyright © 1997 by Susan Marie Swanson. Reprinted by permission of the author. "Haiku," 15. Reprinted with the permission of Atheneum Books for Young Readers, an imprint of Simon & Schuster Children's Publishing Division from *Black Swan, White Crow* by J. Patrick Lewis. Copyright © 1995 J. Patrick Lewis. "Best Friends," 15. Copyright © 1986 Adrian Henri. Reproduced by permission of the estate of Adrian Henri c/o Rogers, Coleridge & White Ltd., 20 Powis Mews, London W11 1JN. "The Tiger," 15. From *Fur, Fangs, and Footprints: A Collection of Poems About Animals* by Patricia Stockland. Copyright © 2004 by Compass Point Books. "Bloodcurdling Screams," 16. From *Technically, It's Not My Fault: Concrete Poems* by John Grandits. Copyright © 2004 by John Grandits. Reprinted by permission of Houghton Mifflin Company. All Rights Reserved. "SweetPea" and "Diamante," 17. Printed by permission of Laura Purdie Salas. "Jacks," 18. From *Lemonade Sun And Other Summer Poems* by Rebecca Kai Dotlich. (Wordsong, an imprint of Boyds Mills Press, Inc. 1998.) Reprinted with the permission of Boyds Mills Press, Inc. Text copyright © 1998 by Rebecca Kai Dotlich. "Hotel Deep, " 19. Excerpt from *Hotel Deep: Light Verse from Dark Water*, copyright © 2005 by Kurt Cyrus, reprinted by permission of Harcourt, Inc. "So," 19. From *Been to Yesterdays: Poems of a Life* by Lee Bennett Hopkins. (Wordsong, an imprint of Boyds Mills Press, Inc. 1995.) Reprinted with the permission of Boyds Mills Press, Inc. Text copyright © 1995 by Lee Bennett Hopkins. "Myrtle," 20. From *Flying at Night: Poems 1965–1985* by Ted Kooser, © 2005. Reprinted by permission of the University of Pittsburgh Press. "The Wind Woman," 20. From *Swing Around the Sun* by Barbara Juster Esbensen. Text copyright © 1965 by Lerner Publications Company, © 2003 by Carolrhoda Books, Inc. Reprinted with the permission of Carolrhoda Books, a division of Lerner Publishing Group, Inc. All rights reserved. "like sun," 21. From *Reaching for Sun*, copyright © 2007 by Tracie Vaughn Zimmer. Reprinted by permission of author. "Shaking," 22, and "Gumeye Ball," 30. From *A Light in the Attic* by Shel Silverstein. Copyright © 1981 by Evil Eye Music, Inc. Used by permission of HarperCollins Publishers. "The Panther," 22. Copyright © 1940 by Ogden Nash, renewed. Reprinted by permission of Curtis Brown, Ltd. "The Coyote," 23. From *Mammalabilia*, copyright © 2000 by Douglas Florian, reprinted by permission of Harcourt, Inc. "El Noche," 24. From *Bronx Masquerade* by Nikki Grimes, copyright © 2002 by Nikki Grimes. Used by permission of Dial Books for Young Readers, A Division of Penguin Young Readers Group, A Member of Penguin Group (USA) Inc., 345 Hudson St. New York, NY 10014. All Rights Reserved. "Hieroglyph," 25. Copyright © 1997 by Ann Turner. Reprinted by permission of Curtis Brown, Ltd. "No No No," 26. Reprinted with permission from *Hugging The Rock* by Susan Taylor Brown. Copyright © 2006 by Susan Taylor Brown, Tricycle Press, Berkeley, CA. www.tenspeed.com. "The Magical Mouse," 27. By Kenneth Patchen, from *The Collected Poems Of Kenneth Patchen*, copyright © 1957 by New Directions Publishing Corp. Reprinted by permission of New Direction Publishing Corp. "Ode to Pablo's Tennis Shoes," 28. From *Neighborhood Odes*, copyright © 1992 by Gary Soto, illustrations copyright © 1992 by David Diaz, reprinted by permission of Harcourt, Inc. "Giraffes," 29. By Sy Kahn. Copyright © 1962 by Sy Kahn. "Mary Had a ...," 30. From *Science Verse* by Jon Scieszka, copyright © 2004 by Jon Scieszka, text. Used by permission of Viking Children's Books, A Division of Penguin Young Readers Group, A Member of Penguin Group (USA) Inc., 345 Hudson St., New York, NY 10014. All rights reserved. "And Stands There Sighing," 31. By Elizabeth Coatsworth. Reproduced with permission from the November 21, 1946, issue of *The Christian Science Monitor* (www.csmonitor.com). © 1946 *The Christian Science Monitor*. All rights reserved. "The New Colossus," Statue of Liberty Inscription," 31. Public domain. "The Ostrich Is a Silly Bird," 31. Public domain. "Puppy Pileup," 32. Printed by permission of Jan Fields. "Hide and Seek," 32. From *The Poor Boy Who Followed His Star and Children's Poems* by Robert Graves. Reprinted by permission of A.P. Watt Ltd. on behalf of the Trustees of The Robert Graves Copyright Trust. "409 (The Battle-Field)," 34. By Emily Dickinson. Public domain. "The Raven," 35. By Edgar Allan Poe. Public domain. "Anapests," 35. Printed by permission of Laura Purdie Salas. *Romeo and Juliet*, 36. By William Shakespeare. Public domain. "Homecoming," 37. © Kathi Appelt. Used with permission of Pippin Properties, Inc. "Into The Mud," 39. From *Song Of The Water Boatman And Other Pond Poems* by Joyce Sidman. Text copyright © 2005 by Joyce Sidman. Reprinted by permission of Houghton Mifflin Company. All rights reserved. "This Is My Rock," 39. From *Every Time I Climb A Tree* by David McCord. Copyright © 1952 by David McCord. By permission of Little Brown & Company. "Primer Lesson," 39. From *Slabs Of The Sunburnt West* by Carl Sandburg, copyright 1922 by Harcourt, Inc. and renewed 1950 by Carl Sandburg, reprinted by permission of the publisher. "When I Was Lost," 40. From *All Together* by Dorothy Aldis, copyright 1925–1928, 1934, 1939, 1952, renewed 1953, © 1954–1956, 1962 by Dorothy Aldis, © 1967 by Roy E. Porter, renewed. Used by permission of G.P. Putnam's Sons, A Division of Penguin Young Readers Group, A Member of Penguin Group (USA) Inc., 345 Hudson St., New York, NY 10014. All rights reserved. "In the Bathtub of Possibilities," 41. Printed by permission of Kelly R. Fineman. "Dog," 42. From *The Cat & the Cuckoo*, published by Roaring Brook Press. and Faber and Faber, Ltd., publishers. Copyright © 2002 by Ted Hughes. All rights reserved. "Child Frightened by a Thunderstorm," 42. From *Official Entry Blank* by Ted Kooser, University of Nebraska Press, 1969, and is here reprinted by permission of the author. "Elephant," 43, 45. From *Animal Poems* by Valerie Worth, pictures by Steve Jenkins. Text copyright © 2007 by George Bahlke. Illustrations copyright © 2007 by Steve Jenkins. Reprinted by permission of Farrar, Straus and Giroux, LLC. "When I Grow Up," 44. From *A Suitcase of Seaweed and Other Poems* by Janet S. Wong. Copyright © 1996 Janet S. Wong. Reprinted by permission of the author. "Doors," 45. From *The Complete Poems Of Carl Sandburg*, Copyright © 1950 by Carl Sandburg and renewed 1978 by Margaret Sandburg, Helga Sandburg Crile and Janet Sandburg, reprinted by permission of Harcourt, Inc.

Further information

Spend time at your school and neighborhood libraries. Talk to the librarians and ask them to recommend poetry for teens. Ask whether they know of magazines that publish young poets. They might know of local organizations that give poetry classes or workshops. Talk to your language arts teacher and ask the same questions.

Go to your local bookstore and browse through the poetry section. Also check the newspaper for the local listings of poetry readings and book signings. Some cities host occasional poetry slams, too. Many authors and poets visit schools and offer writing workshops. Ask your teacher to invite a favorite poet to speak at your school.

On the Web

For more information on this topic, use FactHound.
1. Go to *www.facthound.com*
2. Type in this book ID: 075653519
3. Click on the *Fetch It* button.
FactHound will find the best Web sites for you.

Read all the Write Your Own books

Write Your Own Adventure Story
Write Your Own Autobiography
Write Your Own Biography
Write Your Own Fairy Tale
Write Your Own Fantasy Story
Write Your Own Folktale
Write Your Own Historical Fiction Story
Write Your Own Legend
Write Your Own Mystery Story
Write Your Own Myth
Write Your Own Poetry
Write Your Own Realistic Fiction Story
Write Your Own Science Fiction Story
Write Your Own Tall Tale

Books cited

Aldis, Dorothy. *All Together: A Child's Treasury of Verse*. New York: G.P. Putnam's Sons, 1952.

Appelt, Kathi. *Poems from Homeroom: A Writer's Place to Start*. New York: Henry Holt, 2002.

Bagert, Brod, ed. *Edgar Allan Poe*. New York: Sterling Pub. Co., 1995.

Brown, Susan Taylor. *Hugging the Rock*. Berkeley, Calif.: Tricycle Press, 2006.

Cyrus, Kurt. *Hotel Deep: Light Verse from Dark Water*. New York: Harcourt, Inc., 2005.

Dickinson, Emily. Thomas H. Johnson, ed. *The Complete Poems of Emily Dickinson*. Boston: Little, Brown and Co., 1961.

Dotlich, Rebecca Kai. *Lemonade Sun*. Honesdale, Pa.: Wordsong/Boyds Mills Press, Inc., 1998.

Dotlich, Rebecca Kai. *When Riddles Come Rumbling: Poems to Ponder*. Honesdale, Pa.: Wordsong/Boyds Mills Press, 2001.

Dunning, Stephen, Edward Lueders, and Hugh Smith, eds. *Reflections on a Gift of Watermelon Pickle and Other Modern Verse*. New York: Lothrop, Lee & Shepard, 1967.

Esbensen, Barbara Juster. *Swing Around the Sun*. Minneapolis: CarolRhoda Books, 2003.

Fleischman, Paul. *Joyful Noise: Poems for Two Voices*. New York: HarperTrophy, 2004.

Fletcher, Ralph. *Moving Day*. Honesdale, Pa.: Wordsong/Boyds Mills Press, 2007.

Florian, Douglas. *Comets, Stars, the Moon, and Mars*. San Diego: Harcourt, 2007.

Florian, Douglas. *Mammalabilia: Poems and Paintings*. San Diego: Harcourt, 2000.

Grandits, John. *Technically, It's Not My Fault: Concrete Poems*. New York: Clarion Books, 2004.

Grimes, Nikki. *Bronx Masquerade*. New York: Dial Books, 2002.

Hollyer, Belinda. *She's All That! Poems About Girls*. Boston: Kingfisher, 2006.

Hopkins, Lee Bennett. *Been to Yesterdays: Poems of a Life*. Honesdale, Pa: Wordsong/Boyds Mills Press, 1999.

Hopkins, Lee Bennett, ed. *Marvelous Math: A Book of Poems*. New York: Simon & Schuster Books for Young Readers, 1997

Hopkins, Lee Bennett, ed. *Rainbows Are Made: Poems by Carl Sandburg*. New York: Harcourt, Brace, Jovanovich, 1982.

Hughes, Langston. *The Dream Keeper and Other Poems*. New York: Alfred A. Knopf, 1994.

Hughes, Ted. *The Cat and the Cuckoo*. Brookfield, Conn.: Roaring Brook Press, 2002.

Kennedy, X.J., and Dorothy M. Kennedy. *Knock at a Star: A Child's Introduction to Poetry.* Boston: Little, Brown, 1999.

Kooser, Ted. *Official Entry Blank.* Lincoln: University of Nebraska Press, 1969.

Kooser, Ted. *One World at a Time.* Pittsburgh: University of Pittsburgh Press, 1985.

Lewis, J. Patrick. *Black Swan White Crow.* New York: Atheneum Books for Young Readers, 1995.

McCord, David. *Every Time I Climb a Tree.* Boston: Little, Brown, 1999.

Patchen, Kenneth. *The Collected Poems of Kenneth Patchen.* New York: New Directions Publishing Corp., 1968.

Peters, Lisa Westberg. *Earthshake: Poems from the Ground Up.* New York: Greenwillow Books, 2003.

Scieszka, Jon, and Lane Smith. *Science Verse.* New York: Viking, 2004.

Shakespeare, William. *Romeo and Juliet.* New York: Modern Library, 2001.

Sidman, Joyce. *Song of the Water Boatman and Other Pond Poems.* Boston: Houghton Mifflin, 2005.

Sidman, Joyce. *This Is Just to Say: Poems of Apology and Forgiveness.* Boston: Houghton Mifflin, 2007.

Sidman, Joyce. *The World According to Dog: Poems and Teen Voices.* Boston: Houghton Mifflin, 2003.

Silverstein, Shel. *A Light in the Attic.* New York: Harper & Row Publishers, 1981.

Soto, Gary. *Neighborhood Odes.* San Diego: Harcourt Brace Jovanovich, 1992.

Stockland, Patricia M. *The Free and the Brave: A Collection of Poems About the United States.* Minneapolis: Compass Point Books, 2004.

Stockland, Patricia M. *Fur, Fangs and Footprints: A Collection of Poems About Animals.* Minneapolis: Compass Point Books, 2004.

Swanson, Susan Marie. *Getting Used to the Dark.* New York: DK Publishing, 1997.

Wong, Janet S. *A Suitcase of Seaweed and Other Poems.* New York: Margaret K. McElderry Books, 1996.

Worth, Valerie. *Animal Poems.* New York: Farrar Straus Giroux, 2007.

Yolen, Jane. *Once Upon Ice and Other Frozen Poems.* Honesdale, Pa.: Wordsong/Boyds Mills Press, 1997.

Zimmer, Tracie Vaughn. *Reaching for Sun.* New York: Bloomsbury Children's Books, 2007.

Image credits

Index